In the vibrant town of Bodyville that is thriving and bright, a special team of heroes protect the residents with all their might.

They are the Mighty Mineral Heroes, a cheerful crew, when they are around they'll look after you.

Captain Calcium helps bones and teeth best, Iron Lass gives you some zest. While Zinc Zapper helps when your immune system is put to the test.

Magnesium Magician, has a calming flair, and Potassium Power's heart really does care.

These mighty mineral kids are quite the team, revitalising folks like a dream.

Iron Lass, with energy to spare, helps everyone, everywhere.

She boosts their strength and keeps them awake, fighting fatigue for Bodyville's sake.

Iron Lass also helps your brain, which comes in handy when learning's a pain.

Captain Calcium, strong and bright, builds bones and teeth with all his might.

He fights off cavities that sugar loves to make, so look after that smile for goodness sake.

When at his best he also serves, muscles, blood, heart and nerves.

Potassium Power, heart so true, keeps your heart beating, just like new.

He helps the muscles work just right, ensuring everyone sleeps well at night.

Potassium Power fights fatigue, making him a star player in the league.

Magnesium Magician, calm and wise, relaxes muscles, and heavy sighs.

She soothes the nerves with a magic trick, and assists with giving bad moods the flick.

Magnesium can also stop a craving, it's more than your mind and muscles that she's saving.

Zinc Zapper, quick and keen, boosts the immune system, sight unseen.

He zaps the germs, keeps illness at bay, protecting Bodyville every day.

Zinc Zapper helps you heal and grow strong, so don't go without for very long.

The Mighty Mineral Heroes also ward off the Junk beasts from the east, who push junk feasts, to say the least.

One day, the pesky beasts came into sight, grumpy, frumpy and ready to fight.

They love the foods that can make you sick, it's part of a Junk beasts' super trick.

The Mighty Mineral Heroes run after them fast, with stamina like theirs the chase won't last.

The Junk Beasts get ready to attack, but the Mighty Mineral League fight back.

Combining powers, they create a shield, protecting Bodyville, they never yield.

The shield makes the Junk beasts disappear, hopefully they don't come back until next year!

To avoid getting into strife, make sure these Mighty Minerals are in your life.

There are other hero minerals such as Copper, Iodine and Selenium too – but that's a story for another day, a future tale for you.

Where to Find these Minerals

Minerals come from the soil and foods we eat, a rainbow of fruits and veggies you just can't beat.

Calcium's in yoghurt, kale and cheese, iron's in meat, spinach and peas.

Magnesium's in dark chocolate, nuts and seeds, zinc's in beans and meats to meet your needs.

Potassium's in bananas, coconuts, avocado, and more, there are also plenty of other foods at the store.

Eating well, we get good nutrition, with minerals and vitamins better health comes to fruition.

First edition published in Australia in 2024

ISBN PAPERBACK: 9798335667548 (Amazon)
ISBN PAPERBACK: 9781763713390 (Ingramspark)
ISBN HARDCOVER: 9780646701516

Imprint: Independently published

Authored and edited by Chrissy Harada, images created digitally.

www.sunshinehealthandnutrition.com.au
ABN: 26 249 460 432

Author's Note

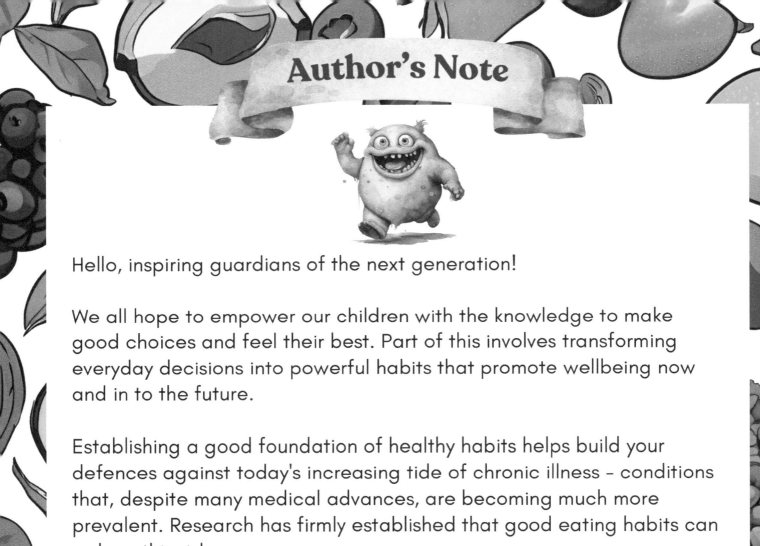

Hello, inspiring guardians of the next generation!

We all hope to empower our children with the knowledge to make good choices and feel their best. Part of this involves transforming everyday decisions into powerful habits that promote wellbeing now and in to the future.

Establishing a good foundation of healthy habits helps build your defences against today's increasing tide of chronic illness – conditions that, despite many medical advances, are becoming much more prevalent. Research has firmly established that good eating habits can reduce this risk.

Together, let's cultivate a generation of healthier super kids, ready to soar into a vibrant future.

Chrissy Harada

About Chrissy

Chrissy Harada is a university qualified nutritionist and journalist, business owner, published writer and mother who is dedicated to promoting the transformative power of good nutrition, especially for young people and mothers.

Her passion for this issue stems from her personal journey of overcoming a number of health challenges by harnessing the benefits of personalised nutrition and cultivating good gut health.

As a nutritionist and mother of three children, including twins, Chrissy understands the crucial role that healthy eating habits play in optimal development, growth, immune system support, disease prevention, and more.

She says health is the real wealth because it becomes the most wanted possession if it is lost.

I would love to hear your thoughts on the book, please leave a review at place of purchase.

Printed in the USA
CPSIA information can be obtained
at www.ICGtesting.com
CBHW060316041024
15321CB00012B/562